At Age Twenty

Maxwell Baumbach

ISBN 978-1-936373-25-3

© 2012 Maxwell Baumbach. All rights reserved. No part of this publication may be reproduced or transmitted in any form or by any means, electronic or mechanical, without permission in writing from the publisher. Requests for permission to make copies of any part of this work should be e-mailed to info@unboundcontent.com.

Published in the United States by Unbound Content, LLC, Englewood, NJ.

Cover art: ©2012, by Jeff Smyers.

The poems in this collection are all original and previously unpublished with the exception of where noted.

At Age Twenty
First edition 2012

For my Mom and Dad; without their continuous support
none of this would be possible.

Table of Contents

Foreword 9
At Age 20 13
From Far Away 14
Grampy's Slots 15
History...16
Blizzard in Chicago 17
Why..18
Kaleidoscopes (an experimental sestina) 20
Voter Registration...22
Harry Caray 23
Harry Baals 24
Zip Lock Lover 25
Better Things 26
Wasted 27
the gods in your eyes 28
Combustion 29
Apples to Oranges 30
You Are Not 31
Secret Genius 32
Sphere Within a Sphere...33
Hero 34
used to be...35
Walking in Fiction 36
Stogies With My CUC Brothers 37
The Sassy Waitress 38
Baby Fat and Naïveté 39
Salesman 40
Mirrors...41
Airplanes 42
My First Open Mic (for Janet Kuypers)........................43
Falling Bird 44
(for Charlie Newman) 45

Tutoring the Lost	46
Poet Laureate	47
In the Dirt	48
My Fantastic Relationship With Christ	49
On the Loss of a Friendship	50
A Glow, a Burning	51
Vanishing Act	52
Parody News	53
Give 'em a Little Credit	54
Boat Racing	55
Wish for You on a Falling Star	56
Fateful Weekends	57
Milk	58
New Glasses	59
Nursing	60
Up All Night	61
The Sun	62
Vegetables	63
My Fifth Birthday	64
Life Without Reason	65
Bikes	66
Childhood Superstar	67
Non-Existent Notes	68
Lemmings	69
The End	70
Holding on	71
You Are So Perfect to Me	72
Alarm Clock	73
Pollen	74
Waiting for the Storm	75
Poor Her	76
Love Is a Luxury	77
Nicholas Sparks Poet	78

Colt Cabana, Pro Wrestler 79
What I Watch 80
Mr. Washington 81
Splinter 82
Daisy 83
Fall, in Love 84
October 85
Reading at the Historic Fine Arts Building in Chicago 86
May God Have Mercy on Your Soul Because I Will Not 87
The Lie of Love and Hate 88
Innocence Lost 89

About the Author 97

Foreword

As a parent, I often consider my children and their friends and wonder what kind of hands we're in as the generations will inexorably turn. There are days when my hopes for a positive time ahead seem dim. And on those days I read a poem by Maxwell Baumbach. Invariably my hope is restored.

Maxwell is the emblem of his generation. He has had all the advantages of growing up in a technological age, he understands the potential for media to entertain, inform, and anesthetize. He is observant, sometimes caustically so, innocent, sometimes brashly so, and tenacious, sometimes cynically so. He is adept at looking askance at the world while trying to find his place within it. His BS detector works very well and he navigates the gray spaces with the moral certainty and personal doubt of youth. Where else would one seek hope in a dark and dismal world?

Maxwell is no stranger to hard work. You will find here the product of innumerable hours of writing, editing, and reading. Dedication to craft is on display from the first poem all the way through the last. In one of our early conversations, Maxwell told me that he continually studies the work of writers he admires to find ways to improve his own writing. There is no better advice I can give as an editor to so motivated a writer. Such a student becomes a master.

In reading this book today you are gaining a glimpse of the immense talent of a representative young man, seeing the creative future as a place of inspiration and illumination. As many times as I have read this book in production, it remains my hopeful read on a dark day. And it whets my appetite for more words from Mr. Maxwell Baumbach. I can't wait to see what he has to say next.

—Annmarie Lockhart, editor

*I have wined and dined
with kings and queens
and
I've slept in alleys
and dined
on pork and beans.*

—Dusty Rhodes

At Age Twenty

Bill Gates
dropped out of Harvard to form Microsoft
DH Lawrence
began writing *The White Peacock*
Plato
became a disciple of Socrates
Jane Austen
wrote *Pride and Prejudice*

and I
pray
that the words
binding this book together
would be held in the same esteem
by someone
somewhere

Maxwell Baumbach

From Far Away

everything looks perfect from far away—
that is why the moon
is heralded for its beauty

it shimmers
   gleams
   glistens
exalting itself from the darkness
of space

enraptured
by its presence
we brought ourselves to the moon
only to promenade along its surface
ridden with craters
           divots
           and unappealing pores

no one
went back
on a second trip

First appeared at Motif, 2011.

At Age Twenty

Grampy's Slots

if I was behaving well
at my grandpa's house
he would take me down to the basement
and let me play on his
quarter slot machine

he would give me a bunch
of quarters
let me drop each one in
and crank the slot

as I watched the whirling fruit
and swirling sevens
I always anticipated
winning

but now
all I can focus on
is what I have lost

Maxwell Baumbach

History

I wish that my history
could be like the internet history
on a computer

I'd hit
control + h
and delete whatever I please

At Age Twenty

Blizzard in Chicago

snow
sweeps
along
city sidewalks
similarly to humans—

lifeless and cold

Maxwell Baumbach

Why

I entered
      the intersection
on a red light
          when my brakes
went out

      as oncoming traffic
sped at me
         I shifted to reverse

no one was behind me

no collisions

         why

was it chance
   that I acted
   the way that I did
   in a given time span

was it the chaos theory
   is my existence
   from this point forward
   the result of a
   butterfly
   thousands of miles away
   not flapping its wings
   hard enough

At Age Twenty

was it God
        divine intervention
                      intervening

I write
    these words
            looking for the answer
                      in a poem

Maxwell Baumbach

Kaleidoscopes (an experimental sestina)

take a look through the   kaleidoscope
  I fucking dare   you
to see this   world
as it is in   reality
not some   distorted
figment of your   imagination

there is not much better than the imagination
it's our own mental   kaleidoscope
choosing things to be   distorted
the god is   you
this is your   reality
your   world

the fantasy is your real   world
a galaxy created by your   imagination
your own   reality
seen through your particular   kaleidoscope
remember the god is   you
you choose how all is   distorted

but even your fantasy becomes   distorted
this is not your ideal   world
and the only one to blame is   you
your fucked up   imagination
your twisted   kaleidoscope
your disappointing   reality

At Age Twenty

is this how you dreamed of   reality
did you think it would all be   distorted
is this how you thought the   kaleidoscope
would reveal the   world
of your   imagination
to   you

it all boils down to   you
and the created   reality
of your   imagination
the   distorted
view you bestowed upon the   world
through the tunnel vision of your   kaleidoscope

the imagination is a gift

but a kaleidoscope reality
leads to a distorted world

Maxwell Baumbach

Voter Registration

I can't wait to vote for the first time

I really like that one politician
who is more charming
than a box of lucky cereal
even though he's just
a political puppet
to attract younger voters
like myself

I can relate to him

but that other guy
who ridicules everyone
that lies and thinks differently than him
is pretty great too

he's smart and understanding

if only life could be easy

At Age Twenty

Harry Caray

I would watch the Cubs games
for the seventh inning stretch

Harry Caray would lean out of the booth
belting the words of "Take Me Out
to the Ball Game"

I was always afraid
that one day
he was going to lean out
too far
and fall to his death
on live television

he did die
but not the way
I had feared

and now
on the rare occasions
I watch a baseball game

I think about those days
from my childhood summers
when I would watch Harry

it always surprises me
how long it has been

Maxwell Baumbach

Harry Baals

there was a vote
to determine the name
for a new government building
that was being erected
in Fort Wayne, Indiana

the runaway winner
of the contest was

The Harry Baals Government Center

Harry Baals
was the former mayor
of the city
but many speculated
that the only reason
his name
was running away with the poll
was because of
its comedic value

and while
many people
laugh it off
or snicker
I am in deep thought
wondering
if I will be remembered
longer
if I change my name
to Ass-Hat McGee

At Age Twenty

Zip Lock Lover

I am your
zip lock lover

pull me out
when it is
convenient
for you

stow me away
at the first sight
of anyone
relevant

all I ask
is that you leave
some
air
inside
the bag

Maxwell Baumbach

Better Things

in your mind
you had better things to do
that summer

better things
than the boy
you kissed goodbye
before you left
for all of June

things like making out
with other boys
after a few shots

in my mind
I had better things to do
than being alive

Wasted

if I had spent every hour
I wasted with you
learning a foreign language
I could have translated the work
of an underappreciated small press poet
from another country
or if I had researched astronomy
I could have made an analogy
about two contrasting constellations
that are burnt out but remain on display
or if I had hit the bottle
I could have at least had an addiction
that motivated me to get out of bed
that dreadful summer

Maxwell Baumbach

the gods in your eyes

your eyes are gods
they make me believe that I am
capable of rising to the greatest depths
of mountains and the heights
that have sunk below seas
unimaginable

they are gods
of that I am convinced when I
look at them to find that my worship
is not enough church should not be
a once a week thing your eyes should be
my lifestyle

each second must belong
to the gods
they will dictate each thought and movement
move me to where they think
I should be at all times
all the time

or so you would have me believe

At Age Twenty

Combustion

combustion
is like dating—

best when spontaneous

Maxwell Baumbach

Apples to Oranges

it is said
that when two things
cannot be compared
a case of apples to oranges exists

but those things can be compared
they are both fruits
and like humans
they have skin
and humans like trees
can be cut down
and trees like flowers
can bend in the wind
and flowers like hummingbirds
can astonish with their beauty
and the hummingbird sings
the way all the earth does

in harmonious unison

At Age Twenty

You Are Not

you are not
the apple of my eye (whatever the hell that even means)
you are not
the constellation that hovers above
you are not
the setting sun of simmering summer's night
you are not
the chandelier
you are not
the angel on top of the Christmas tree

nor are you
the exhausted imagery of poets past

you are a human
that accepts me
and gives me a love
no one else could

for that

you are perfect

regardless of flaws

Secret Genius

when I uncovered
the not so discrete
second meaning of a poem
in my Writing About Literature
class
the girl behind me whispered
"it's like he's a secret genius
or something"

oh
it's not sercet

damn it

I meant
secret

At Age Twenty

Sphere Within a Sphere

I saw a sculpture
in Ireland
of the new world
emerging from the old one

it is not the
now rusting gold
or the curvature
of the spheres
that made it so wondrous

but rather
that this sculpture
will be perpetually relevant

Maxwell Baumbach

Hero

every kid
has their hero
that they chase

aiming to be just like them

mine was
Chris Benoit

a pro wrestler
who accomplished his goals
in the United States
Canada
Mexico
and Japan
despite the projections
that he could not do it

he
murdered his wife
and son
before taking his own life
to escape the consequences

leaving me with nothing
to chase
except for
the acceptance
that my hero
was a coward

At Age Twenty

used to be

you told me I am not as hopeful as I used to be
and while it is a bit unsettling to hear
I guess I can see where you are coming from

today I saw a dead butterfly on the ground
wings stacked on top of one another
and I couldn't stop laughing

it was such a hopeful shade of purple

Maxwell Baumbach

Walking in Fiction

Hillary Clinton
made comments to the media
about how pro-wrestling
is anti-American

which is funny

because she didn't have a problem
going on WWE Raw
to promote her political campaign
during the 2008 Presidential election

it goes to show
that she is as real
as the sport she shits on

At Age Twenty

Stogies With My CUC Brothers

the quality cigar
resonates

filling my mouth
like sound in an amphitheater
the walls of my cheeks
providing
ideal acoustics

the taste
still welcome
hours after
the curtains have closed

Maxwell Baumbach

The Sassy Waitress

she makes witty remarks
to pass the time
the goddamn time
that won't tick
off the clock
fast enough
so that she can leave
and be miserable
in the comfort
of her own home
    instead

At Age Twenty

Baby Fat and Naiveté

as I grow older
I try to shed the things
of childhood

I can stop playing games with my army men—
that is no issue

I can put a halt
to blatant disobedience
for disobedience's sake

I am dropping the baby fat
bit by bit
with proper exercise
and calorie counting

but this naiveté?
this goddamn naiveté?

this unwarranted belief
in others
is eating away at me
like I used to eat away
at a PB&J on white bread

Salesman

my dad is a salesman
so was his dad
and so was his dad's dad

I think I received
that trait
also

I can always
talk people
into coming to the Improv show
to watch me perform
or
going down to the wrestling show
with me
or
whatever else
I please

but I can never
sell me
on myself

At Age Twenty

Mirrors

we paint self-portraits
   in the mirror
each morning

our canvas
   blank
     our mind
       filled with ideas
     of what
   to paint
and how

a mirror
   blank
     empty of
       all ideas
     so we
   impose
our own
image

that we have been taught to see
       in the mirror
despite what we truly are

and no matter how hard
the mirror
or anyone else
tries
the picture always comes out
slightly distorted

Maxwell Baumbach

Airplanes

I used to think that love
was like
jumping out of an airplane

I had to trust
that everything would work out

and I would land safely
on the ground below

but now I think that love
is like
riding on an airplane

and it lands smoothly

just as I knew it would

despite mild turbulence
from time to time

At Age Twenty

My First Open Mic
(for Janet Kuypers)

"Great job!
You can grab yourself a beer
from the bar
and relax until the feature."

"I'm 19."

"Oh.
Well then
don't grab yourself a beer."

Maxwell Baumbach

Falling Bird

one summer at lake geneva
I found a bird on the ground
unable to fly away but still fidgeting

I informed my sisters of it
and they informed our parents

we called him "Falling Bird"
and we fed him
trying to get him back on his feet
momentarily
only to soar back
to wherever it was he fell from

but he died the next day

his heart gave up on him
the way ours does
to all of us
as we grow older

At Age Twenty

(for Charlie Newman)

if a poem
needs a title
or a title fits the poem
give it a title

but if the poem doesn't need a title

don't title it
untitled

just don't give it a title
at all

this poem
up until this stanza
is a quote from Charlie Newman
but I can't put it in quotes
because he dislikes grammar
(BURN GRAMMAR)

shit
I just used parentheses
anything that is my own content
in this poem
is terrible

thus
it does not deserve a title

Maxwell Baumbach

Tutoring the Lost

when I read a poem
for the basic writing class
I tutored in
a student told me
"your shit's dope"

I knew they were lost
when I had to explain to them
that my fecal matter
was not indeed
marijuana

At Age Twenty

Poet Laureate

I want to be Poet Laureate of the United States
when I'm about
oh
let's say 45

I want to be seen on television
approaching the podium as
Vice President Ryan Seacrest
announces me
to the world

at that precise moment
one of my classmates
from high school
will spit out
their overpriced Starbucks coffee
turn to their spouse
and say

"that was the asshole that yelled
'JENGA'
when we watched a video about
a stadium being torn down!"

Maxwell Baumbach

In the Dirt

everyone around me grew tall
                                    thin
                                    fit
they extended
                                    upward

toward the sun
and bloomed
    bodacious

I remained in the dirt
hoping to catch drops
of life-giving water
that somehow slipped
past their petals

At Age Twenty

My Fantastic Relationship With Christ

Hey God
remember when you said,
"Jacob have I loved
but Esau have I hated"

then you told us
not to hate our neighbor
but love them

let's hope you can
forgive me

Maxwell Baumbach

On the Loss of a Friendship

I don't look at it
as losing a friend

I look at it
as gaining
negative one friend

At Age Twenty

A Glow, a Burning

we simultaneously flee from each other
in the same direction

scattering sidewalks
with blazing photographs
of one another

there is no longer
a glow
a burning

we continue
to move parallel

Maxwell Baumbach

Vanishing Act

I see you for a quarter of a second
every time I turn a corner quickly

you are
there
but then
you are gone

like a childhood dream

Parody News

parody news websites
and TV shows
probably supply
a more accurate account of things
than the traditional
"reputable" sources

I too
switched
to the parodies
because at least they can make me smile
and
temporarily
forget that the shit
is approximately 1 cm
away from the fan

Maxwell Baumbach

Give 'em a Little Credit

currency in the United States
is no longer backed by anything

and most people don't even use
the literal paper currency

instead
credit is the avenue of choice

soon
paper money won't exist

how can an economy
fluctuate without actual money

or
a backing system

you
ask;

a currency fairy
will be created—

ruling over
all economic issues

the politicians
who put the fairy in power

remarkably
still backed
by people

At Age Twenty

Boat Racing

as a young boy
I sat on the end
of the pier
at my grandparent's
lake geneva
cottage
watching
boats
race
against one another

floating through the water
like tall pale underweight
rubber duckies

as a college student
I sat on
a floating raft
at a michigan
cottage
with my friends
throwing beer bottles
in the water

the glass bottlenecks
barely above the water
put to shame
by the sailboats
of my childhood

Maxwell Baumbach

Wish for You on a Falling Star

there are millions of stars
in the sky
so I would feel
like I wasn't doing much
if I wished for you
on just
one of them

especially
if it was in the process
of falling on its ass

by the time
we look at the stars
they have already
died

the other stars have
been to the funeral
and attended the luncheon
afterward

it does not seem sensible
to wish for you
on a dead light bulb
millions of miles away

because what we have
I don't want to die

At Age Twenty

Fateful Weekends

I remember a fateful Sunday
when I was seven

at church
I pulled on the coat
of a woman
who I would have sworn
was my mother

oops

and last Saturday
I sucked every last droplet
of booze
from a bottle of Mike's Hard

again
in the wrong place
for what I was looking

Maxwell Baumbach

Milk

milk tasted different when I was a child

poured by my mother
into the cup
with plastic fish on it
handed to me
with a smile
and a pat on the back

New Glasses

need a new pair of glasses

I am not growing any more
all of my clothes fit me
no more hand me downs
yet I still speak
of the future
as if somehow
it will be different
than today and that
when I grow up
even though I supposedly
already have
life will be everything
I dreamed it to be

but the future
is only the past
undiscovered

so I need to take off
these damn glasses
and stop seeing the world
through the lens of a child

Maxwell Baumbach

Nursing

after sneaking onto the roof of the apartment
my friends and I
break out the scotch and cigars

they drink from fancy glasses
like my dead relative had
while I drink mine from a used soda bottle
that still contains traces
of high fructose corn syrup

I think about how nineteen years ago
I was nursed from a bottle
and how I nurse a bottle
and in nine years
I'll nurse someone who drinks from a bottle
but that's merely the cycle of things
and to make anything more out of it
would be overly sentimental

First appeared at Ink, Sweat, and Tears, *November 21, 2011.*

At Age Twenty

Up All Night

there's something about
being awake when everyone else
is asleep

not the sunrise
but the pre-sunrise
when an odd
purple hue
starts to crawl its way
up the atmosphere
opposite another
odd purple hue
that is almost the same
but somehow different
retreating
in the most glorious game
of hide and seek
this world could know

Maxwell Baumbach

The Sun

I act like it is hard
to be alone
even when I am only alone
for a few hours
or days

but I do not know what it is like
to be the sun

chasing after a
constantly fleeing
moon

having to be put on display
eternally alone
for the whole universe
to see

At Age Twenty

Vegetables

when I worked with kids
one summer
there was this boy
who never ate his vegetables

he would get so upset
over it
too

it was like asking
a nazi
to come to terms
with communism

I never understood
how he could get
so riled up
over the issue
every day

then
one afternoon
on the drive home
someone in a large
SUV cut off
my poor purple minivan
(please don't judge me)

and I may have stuck up
a certain finger at him
(see above parentheses)

outraged over something
as petty as peas

Maxwell Baumbach

My Fifth Birthday

my aunt asks me
if I have grown out of Power Rangers
yet

these things take time
I try to explain
but the world does not cease
leaving its oversized handprints on my back
shoving me
onward

this sets in
as I take a long drag
from my candy cigarette

At Age Twenty

Life Without Reason

you ask yourself
why things need to be
a certain way
or why they happen

turn to the constellations
as those before you did

and ask
where are Orion's pants?

Maxwell Baumbach

Bikes

I never rode bikes

it disinterested me
to the point
that I had no desire to learn

my exercise
would be going to the track
with my dad
and running around
the giant oval
like an overweight hamster
stuck in its wheel

yesterday
I walked through a forest preserve

I wanted to turn the page
of scenery
to see what nature
had in store
next

making me wonder
about the bike rides past
that I had missed

At Age Twenty

Childhood Superstar

my dad would pass me the ball
with five seconds left
in our basketball game
against invisible opponents

I would take a jump shot from
eight feet out

if I made it
we won

and if I missed
he would tip it in
and we would win anyway

but that never put a damper on the excitement
when he would pick me up
after a victory

we would celebrate

pandering to a cheering audience
of clouds

Maxwell Baumbach

Non-Existent Notes

I do not know
how to play
the guitar
or
the ukelele

but I sit on this
Eldridge Park hill
plucking away
at the invisible strings
of poetry

At Age Twenty

Lemmings

false information
was released
in the 1950s
that lemmings
jump off of cliffs

inadvertently committing
mass suicide

however
workers on the documentary
that filmed this event
admitted that the lemmings
were placed in unfamiliar territory
and guided off
to produce the scene

no one kills themselves
on their own

The End

after spending his entire life
"thinking outside
of the box"
they throw him
into a box
throw the box
into the ground
and throw dirt
on the box
while his family
watches on

happily ever after

At Age Twenty

Holding on

I don't know why I bother
holding onto things

they always seem
to slip from my grasp
like leaves
hopelessly trying
to clutch the summer breeze
before the fall
has its way with them

if something does
stay sheltered
between my knuckles and palms

I will clench my hands
until death

covered in dirt
still holding on
with no purpose

Maxwell Baumbach

You Are So Perfect to Me

that even the
patterns of your breaths
sound like a flawless
wind symphony

At Age Twenty

Alarm Clock

today
I did not wake up
until my alarm clock
    stopped making noise

so maybe
if we all
shut the hell up
    for a minute

the world can
smell the coffee

Maxwell Baumbach

Pollen

I envisioned you by the shore that summer
picking daffodils from the grass
that the water washes up to
and blowing the pollen that is then
blown by the wind

I envision the pollen floating through the air
from California to my feet
here in Elmhurst

bits of breath
still present

At Age Twenty

Waiting for the Storm

locked in the
basement
waiting
for the
storm
to
blow over
the way
the rest of my life
already has

Maxwell Baumbach

Poor Her

her beauty
must be
such a
hindrance

the way
she complains
about
being checked out
and how she hates
guys looking at her
when she works out
in short shorts
with full make-up on

if only
she could just
be ugly
like everyone else

At Age Twenty

Love Is a Luxury

love
is a luxury
that can be afforded
by anyone
willing to lay down
the hefty payment
of their own
selfish desires

Maxwell Baumbach

Nicholas Sparks Poet

I wish I could be the
Nicholas Sparks
of poetry

I would write a bunch of poems
that are completely interchangeable

unrealistic characters
creating
even less realistic expectations
of romance

same formula
different character plugged in
locations varied

I would make
millions of dollars
for each one

they would make
movies
about them

and
my lack of evolution
would create another argument
for intelligent design

Colt Cabana, Pro Wrestler

he could have been
a salesman
a doctor
or a comedic actor
he explains
but instead
he is a freak show

he puts on a singlet
and brawls

he punches
wallops
bleeds

and
more than anything
entertains

painting masterpieces
on a canvas
between four ropes
more beautiful
than the work
of most artists

as he comes back through the curtain
he peels off his wrist tape
shakes the hand of his opponent
unlaces his boots

just another day on the job

Maxwell Baumbach

What I Watch

my favorite episodes of television shows
are the season finales—
where everything in a person's life
seems to wrap up perfectly
like a present
on a holiday

my favorite movies are the teen romance ones
where they go to the prom—
when everything in a person's life
turns from steaming shit
to the shining shimmering splendor
of a whole new world

those are my favorites
because life is not a
season finale
or
prom night

gifts are not wrapped up perfectly
but sufficiently

and steaming shit
can only turn into
lukewarm crap

At Age Twenty

Mr. Washington

we stand
    in a pit
deeper than the
      grandest of canyons
with waterfalls
      cascading their substance
down at us
    from every angle

drowning
    in the place we have built ourselves
we turn to Mr. Washington
        in desperation
asking
   what not he can do
for himself
    but what he can do for his nation

with a smile
    that gleams of freshly cleaned pearls
he tells us
    hope

we bellow screams
      of triumph
toot the horns
      of ourselves

the water that drowns us
          still flowing

Splinter

I am a sliver
of a splinter
in the universe
but it is my dream
that the words
I write
will create
a visible bruise

At Age Twenty

Daisy
(based on a girl from the documentary "Waiting for Superman")

sorry
Daisy

no quality education
for you

you have been bound
by geographical boundaries
and born into
the wrong family
so you don't get the same opportunities
as others

good luck paying for college

Maxwell Baumbach

Fall, in Love

after picking out our respective pumpkins
we gut the poor bastards
savagely ripping out their innards
not unlike what we have done
to each other

ruthlessly removing
slimy orange baggage
and replacing it with a candle

illuminating love

At Age Twenty

October

letterman jackets and high school football
trouncing burnt orange leaves
fingers tied together like hostages

hearts hostage
to the thought
that this is forever

college will come
like a surgeon's scissors

cutting out
vital parts
of current life

Maxwell Baumbach

Reading at the Historic Fine Arts Building in Chicago

there is not much
that is more frightening
than reading poetry
in front of people
that actually matter

they look at me
probably thinking

"who the hell is this kid?"
"does he think he belongs here?"
"what the hell did he eat to become that large?"

in my first poem
I joke
that I am a dumbass

laughter fills the room
applause settles me down

At Age Twenty

May God Have Mercy on Your Soul Because I Will Not

I have listened to you
talk about your ex-boyfriend
and how you are
SUFFERING
to everyone who would listen
for the last seven hours

tell me how your food tastes
how your sixty dollar sweatshirt keeps you warm in the cold
how it feels to be healthy
how your parents are still together

forget the starving kids in Ethiopia
the tormented homosexuals in Iran
the oppressed citizens of Libya
the white farmers of Zimbabwe
the families who lost their children to cancer
the teenage girls with eating disorders
the Katrina victims still in debt
and the homeless in Atlanta

because they don't know SUFFERING
like you do
honey

Maxwell Baumbach

The Lie of Love and Hate

There are so many songs about love
falling for something beautiful
a focal point of our culture
the world is fixated on it

we are always taught that hate is wrong
a destructive evil
that tears everything apart
nothing is worse

we are told this is true
but love has hurt me
more than hate ever could

At Age Twenty

Innocence Lost

I. The Girl on the Cruise

on the deck
beneath the stars
my lips met their first friends

they belonged to
girl one
a Boston native
with wicked blond hair
and a smile
as naive as mine

my friend
said she had big teeth
but how picky can you be
as a chubby fourteen year old

months later
we argued over the phone
and I haven't heard her voice
since

II. Dance

I wanted to dance
with girl two

twirl her about
and swing her around

Maxwell Baumbach

despite the fact
I didn't know how

she twirled and swung
with someone else

III. Leaning on an Invisible Wall

I was fascinated with
girl three

I could not shake her
from my head
for more than a few seconds
before she crawled back
onto the thought train

and despite
all the time I devoted to her
I never understood
why I was stuck on her

to this day
I still don't

constant mistreatment
verbal abuse
cutting me down

At Age Twenty

belief in myself
a dependent
on an outside party
that did not give a damn

IV. Girl Four

I will not give
girl four
the time of day
since she broke things off
through text

she didn't have the courtesy
to give me
a phone call

I don't have the courtesy
to give the afterthought of her
a well-written poem

V. The Psycho

girl five
was adamant about the fact
that we could never work

but two months later
was even more adamant about the fact
that we could make it work

Maxwell Baumbach

I was too broken down
to put myself
together again
only to be broken back down

VI. Scum

girl six
dated me
an entire summer
before breaking things off
out of nowhere

she still doesn't know
that I know
about the other guy
she saw the entire time

fuckin' harlot
scum of the earth
I hope reincarnation exists
so that I can come back
as a bird
to shit in her purse

VII. The Life Changer

she didn't make me
give up a damn thing

At Age Twenty

she never tried to impress me
so I never tried back

I almost shat my pants
when she grabbed my hand

halfway through watching Fight Club
I paused it

to ask her out
because I'm classy like that

she said yes
and we kissed

my innocence was gone
sure

but she gave me
peace of heart

stability
fulfillment

belief
LOVE

and
more than anything

Maxwell Baumbach

the knowledge
that this will be

my final
chapter

happily
ever after

MAXWELL BAUMBACH is quite the character. He grew up in Lisle IL and Elmhurst IL, attending Timothy Christian School from third grade through the end of high school. It was there that he got an education both in and out of the classroom. He was blessed with outstanding teachers and the opportunity to participate in athletics. While at Timothy he played basketball, track and field, and even men's volleyball. Through sports and writing, he learned about things beyond what textbooks could teach. A series of horribly failed relationships also aided in the process. He is currently a college student at Concordia University, where he is a sports management major. He was paired with an equally out-there roommate, Phillip Cooper, who is partially responsible for Maxwell becoming even more strange. He has been dating his girlfriend, Kristina, for two years and he hopes to be with her forever. His family has been unbelievably supportive of him. Both sets of grandparents, Carol and Don and Emil and Lynn, his parents, Mark and Kim, his sisters, Heidi and Allie, and his nephew Zach are constant sources of motivation for him. If everyone else in his family wasn't as successful and cool as they are, he wouldn't have anything to chase.